Hush, The Lord Is Talking
and Other True Tales

By
Dr. C. Ronald S. Williams II
Pastor and Senior Elder
Mount Zion Fellowship of the Brethren

Illustrations by Nancy Robinson

Edited by Roger Morton and Robert Delancy

CHRISTIAN • LITERATURE • CRUSADE
Fort Washington, Pennsylvania 19034

These tales are true.
They are based on the experiences
of my life,
shared, as they were,
with those closest to me
at that past time,
in that special place.
With deepest love and affection,
these stories are dedicated to
my mother and father,
Dr. and Mrs. St. Clare Williams,
my sisters, Rosalyn and Saundra,
my aunts and uncles,
my cousins
who are friends, too, in my mind,
and above all, to my grandparents,
Ollie and Lela McAdams.

MAMA IS HOME

he evening before the morning when Mama was to come home, I was filled with anticipation and excitement. I was looking forward to seeing my Mama.

Due West, South Carolina, was home to everyone in the McAdams clan. My grandparents had seven children who survived to adulthood. Four of them had moved to different parts of the country.

Two of their daughters lived in Cleveland, Ohio, one in Far Rockaway, New York, another in Washington, D.C., and one, Aunt Francis, was at home with my grandparents in South Carolina. Each summer, everyone would meet in Due West.

Life seemed good and I did not have a care, other than trying to be a good child.

I had been home for about a month, having the time of my life with my cousins and my dear grandparents. Always, though, there was something missing because Mama was not with me. She was still in Cleveland with Daddy.

I guess I had always been a "Mama's Boy." When she was not around, I missed her. But, she was going to be home the next day.

I was a little nervous about her seeing me, because she had told me to stay

2

3

out of the woods. But I couldn't help myself, I loved the woods.

Now that Mama was coming, I was a bit uneasy, because I had gotten into some poison ivy in the woods and was covered with the purple medicine my grandmother put on me to stop the itching. I did not want Mama to see it.

Everyone was excited, because their Aunt Pearl—that's my Mama—was coming home. I think that even the chickens were excited. They had not done their "business" in the backyard after we had swept it.

Yes, we did sweep the backyard. The backyard was nothing but dirt. So, we were sweeping dirt.

We made the dirt look good by sweeping away all of the chicken droppings and twigs that had fallen from the pecan tree in a storm that day.

I was known as the Chicken Boy, because I loved to chase and catch them. I got some of the worst spankings of my life because of those chickens.

I had trouble falling asleep that night. I could not wait for the morning. The train was scheduled to arrive in Abbeville at 5:50 in the morning, and I knew that when I woke up Mama would be home.

I heard the grown-ups early the next morning as they left the house. I heard the car start up and listened as it moved down the rocky dirt road that lay between the big house and the highway.

I could not go back to sleep after they left, because I knew they were going to get Mama.

An hour later, I heard the car coming up the driveway.

I jumped out of bed.

It was the break of day.

Mama was home.

As the front door opened, I ran down the long center hall and jumped into her arms. After she hugged and kissed me, she looked at me and asked, "Boy, what's wrong with your face?"

I was so happy to see her, it didn't matter what she said or how she said it. Mama was home!

I have used that experience in my life to try to imagine how wonderful it is going to be when all of God's children get home.

Jesus said, "I go to prepare a place for you. And if I go and prepare a place for you, I will come again, and receive you unto Myself; that where I am, there ye may be also." (John 14:2–3)

It's almost the break of day.

I am excited about seeing Him come through the door of the skies.

I am excited about going home.

MOUNT ZION

*I*t never ceases to amaze me how childhood experiences come to influence our attitudes through adolescence and on into adulthood. I gained some of those very experiences at Mount Zion Presbyterian Church. It was a wonderful place for me.

Sometimes I think I must have been born in church. At Mount Zion, there was preaching every first and third Sunday, and Sunday School every second and fourth Sunday.

The church was always filled with my relatives—grandparents, aunts, uncles, first cousins, second cousins, third cousins, and every other kind of cousin. It seemed as though we were all related to each other in some way.

After Sunday School, we would go to the outhouse. Boys went to their outhouse and girls to theirs. We would swap bubble gum and chew rabbit tobacco we had picked in the fields.

All of the McAdams grandchildren sang in the choir and my cousin Roberta played the piano.

Every Sunday, my grandfather would give each of us three pennies to put into the Sunday School collection. I always put mine in the offering plate. I can't say the same for my cousins.

One first Sunday in particular stands out in my mind. Reverend Hanes was going to preach. We were all in the choir stand. The hymn of preparation was "Faith of Our Fathers." Roberta played the introduction and we began to sing. But something was wrong. I had never heard Roberta sing before and now I understood why.

Roberta sounded like a fog horn in the key of "don't try it." We couldn't sing because we were laughing so hard. Roberta continued to make that noise.

She was getting happier by the minute, singing the hymn. We were about to die from laughing. At last, after we had sung all of the verses of the hymn, a strange hush fell over the congregation as Reverend Hanes approached the pulpit.

The Reverend looked over the congregation, then he spoke. "Well, the Good Book says, 'Let everything that hath breath praise the Lord.' I guess that includes everybody, too."

We thought we would fall down laughing, because things like that just didn't happen at Mount Zion Presbyterian. After that Sunday I never heard Roberta sing again. Thank God!

Since that time, I have come to appreciate even the sound of a fog horn, as long as the sound is giving praise to God. Psalm150:6 ever reminds us to "Let everything that hath breath praise the Lord."

After service, we'd all pile into trucks, cars, and sometimes a horse and buggy, and go home to a big Sunday dinner. We were not allowed to do any work on Sunday, because that was the Lord's day.

As I reflect on those days, I can still remember going outside after dinner and getting lost in the big pine woods that lay beyond the pasture behind the big house.

Those trees were so stately, so regal as they pointed toward the sky declaring the glory of God. The birds sang in evening praise and the wind gently reminded me that there is Somebody bigger than I.

He deserves my praise.

"Let everything that hath breath praise the Lord."

GOING FISHING

s children, we were blessed to have a grandfather who we thought could do everything. Grandfather was a man of great wisdom and a very practical man, as well. Yes, Ollie McAdams, Sr., was a great man.

Grandfather was an excellent hunter, farmer, fisherman, and bird dog trainer—just to mention a few of his accomplishments.

However, more important than any of that, he was a great father, grandfather, and man of God.

I loved to watch him work the fields with his mule. He would plant enough wheat to provide us with flour all through the winter.

Grandfather would kill enough hogs to fill the smokehouse and supply the family with meat all year.

He taught us how to milk the cows, churn the butter, slop the hogs, work the fields, hunt squirrels, rabbits, and partridge. He taught us our Bible verses, and how to shine our shoes. These were only a handful of the many things he taught us about so many different parts of life.

My most enjoyable times with Grandfather were when he would cut some bamboo poles. Then I would know that he was getting ready to take us fishing.

After he would prepare the poles and furnish them with a fishing line, we would go to the cow manure heap and dig worms. Although it wasn't a very pleasant job, it yielded a lot of worms. Then we were ready to go fishing.

We would walk through many different parts of pastures, fields, and woods on our way to one of Grandfather's secret fishing holes. He would walk silently while we ran and jumped with excitement as we moved along the way. When Grandfather would softly, yet firmly, say, "Hush," we knew we were close to where we would fish.

One of the fishing trips in particular sticks in my mind. Grandfather had taken us to a creek on the back side of Mr. Bowie's land. Mr. Bowie owned a lot of property that was riddled with creeks.

When we arrived, there was a place where the creek was widest and deepest. Here the water was crystal clear. We could actually see the fish through the water. They were everywhere.

There were stripped fish, yellow fish, green fish, little fish, big fish—all of them were in the place where the water was deepest and the creek was widest.

We baited our hooks and dropped our lines into the water. Everyone was catching fish. I hooked a fish so big that when I finally yanked it out of the water, it flew through the air and smacked me in the face.

I was not pleased about that, but Grandfather smiled at me, so I was proud of myself and my big fish.

That day we caught fish where the creek was widest and deepest.

Many of us who have a belief in the Lord Jesus Christ for our salvation have not caught many fish because we have been fishing in shallow places.

In the Apostle Paul's prayer for the Ephesians, he hoped, "That Christ may dwell in your hearts by faith; that ye, being rooted and grounded in love, may be able to comprehend with all the saints what is the breadth, and length, and depth, and height; and to know the love of Christ, which passeth knowledge, that ye might be filled with all the fullness of God." (Ephesians 3:17–19)

It is only as we go deep into God that joy can be realized in our deepest sorrow, peace can be felt in the midst of great confusion, assurance can be felt when all around us is shaky.

Let us go fishing in deep places.

BLACKBERRIES, APPLES, PEACHES AND PEARS

ave you ever heard the old saying, "living off the fat of the land"? Well, believe me when I tell you that in Due West we lived off the fat of the land.

In their seasons, we picked blackberries, apples, peaches, pears, muscadines, figs, and whatever else was around. There were pecan trees, black walnut trees, and even peanuts hanging out to dry.

Every now and then, my cousins and I were able to sneak a watermelon from Grandfather's patch. But whenever we were caught doing that, he lit up our behinds!

My grandmother canned everything, and when the fruits ripened, we all got busy. Some picked. Some peeled. Some cut up. Some cooked. Some canned. Everyone worked. The work was hard, but the rewards were sweet.

My grandmother made the best blackberry and peach cobblers this side of heaven. Her apple pie and pear preserves were the best, too. My job was to pick the fruit. I didn't mind picking, except for one thing. I hated those yellow jackets. We would find those stinging

15

devils wherever fruit was rotting on the ground. It seemed as though they wanted to prevent us from getting what we thought was rightfully ours.

One day, while we were picking pears, a yellow jacket flew up my Cousin Bubba's pant leg and began to sting him.

Bubba pulled off his pants right there and began to run around the yard, yelping every step of the way. We could hardly work after that because every time we looked at Bubba, we would fall down laughing.

After Bubba put his pants back on, he took some string and tied up the bottom of both his pant legs. Then he put on a long-sleeve shirt, buttoning it to the top. Bubba even put a hat on his head. He was covered from head to toe. He continued to work, rubbing his wounds every now and then.

Later that day, we began to tease Bubba about the incident. Bubba's only response was, "Dem bees wasn't gonna stop me from gettin' my preeeserves."

As I reflect back on that day, I think how wonderful it would be if we would not allow a few stings in life to prevent us from "getting our preserves."

"Above all, taking the shield of faith, wherewith ye shall be able to quench all the fiery darts of the wicked." (Ephesians 6:16)

Bubba was covered from head to toe. Our only defense from the fiery darts of the evil one is to be covered from head to toe, too.

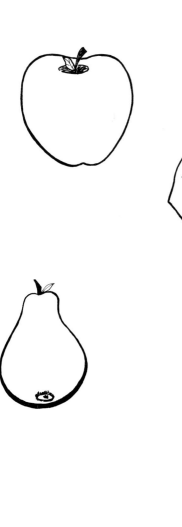

17

DISCIPLINE

y grandfather was an equal opportunity disciplinarian. When one of us had disobeyed and gotten in trouble, all of us had to pay for it, because we would not tell Grandfather who the culprit really was.

There was a day, for instance, when my cousins Willie and Franklyn had taken one of Grandfather's watermelons out of the patch and eaten it. They had tried to give me some of it, but I would not take it. I really had wanted some of that melon, but I knew that if I had eaten some of it, I would be just as guilty as they were.

Later that day, my grandfather went out to weed the watermelon patch. I was hoping he wouldn't notice the missing melon, but he did.

I watched him as he slowly walked back to the big house with a "I'm-going-to-whip-somebody" look on his face. The only three people that knew what had happened were Willie, Franklyn, and me.

Grandfather came into the house and asked, "Who did it?"

My grandmother asked, "Did what?"

Grandfather continued, "Somebody took my prize melon out of the

watermelon patch. I want to know who did it!"

Well, no one opened their mouth. This irritated Grandfather, so he called all of us into the backyard, where he proceeded to pull out his pocket knife and cut a switch off of the peach tree.

Next he began to take the leaves off of the switch and worked until it became a mighty weapon. He lined us up from the oldest to the youngest. I was one of the younger ones, so I was near the end of the line.

I knew that if I told who did it, my cousins would beat me up. So I held my peace.

As Grandfather began to spank the first of my cousins in the line, I began to wonder if it was going to be worth me holding my peace. The closer he came to me, the closer I got to telling who did it.

Suddenly, I was next in line and I yelled "Willie and Frank did it, Grandfather!" I blurted it out before I even knew I had spoken.

Everyone in line behind me was relieved and happy. Everyone in line in front of me was very upset with me.

I thought I had been saved from impending doom when suddenly Grandfather spanked me anyway. While he was spanking me he said, "You should have told me earlier."

As might be imagined, my cousins didn't play with me for a couple of days, and I was an outcast for telling on them.

After my grandfather had spanked me, I wished I had gone on and eaten some of that watermelon, but it was too late for that. The fact is, all of us were punished for the bad decision of a few.

I have learned that we need to consider our actions before we act. There are many issues in life which we must think through carefully before we act or react. Remember, the decision that we make today could affect many people tomorrow.

After that day and its lesson, I had learned how to stay out of Trouble's Way. If I saw someone doing something that had the potential of getting all of us into trouble, I did everything I could to persuade them not to do it.

After all, Grandfather knew how to use a peach-tree hickory.

GRANDMOTHER'S BISCUITS

6

Our family was the type that would gather around the breakfast table to discuss the issues of the day.

We would wake up every moming with the aroma of coffee perking, the scent of country ham, sausage, bacon, or scrapple frying, and the wonderful fragrance of biscuits baking.

There was loud talk to be heard, too. My Uncle Ollie had a loud, booming voice. When he laughed, it seemed to shake the whole house.

The kitchen was our meeting place. Grandmother's kitchen was the largest room in the house and everyone gathered there.

When I woke up, there were chores to be done. One of my chores was to empty the chamber pots. I hated that job!

Since we didn't have indoor plumbing at the time, each bedroom had a pot in which we did our business during the night. About the time I finished emptying the chamber pots, everyone would begin to gather in the kitchen for breakfast.

Adults would sit at one table and the children usually sat at another. Then my grandfather would take his seat at the head of the table and bless the food. I would love to hear my grandfather pray. But there were times he prayed

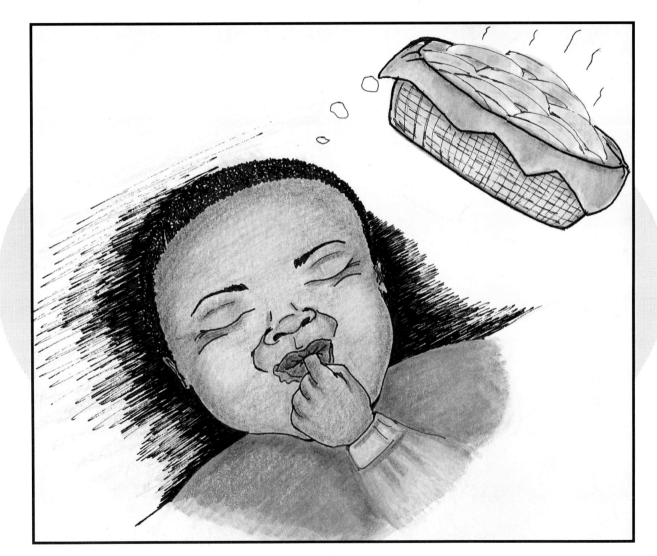

so long that rigor mortis set in on the grits.

Then, everyone would begin to dive in on the food. I couldn't wait to get to the biscuits. Grandmother's biscuits were not thick. They were thin, hot, and good.

We would take homemade preserves and jelly, as well as the home-churned butter, and we'd slap them on the biscuits. Talk about good—that stuff was good! Grandmother would always make more than enough biscuits, in case someone would get hungry before dinner. We always did.

After breakfast, we would take the biscuits and put jelly on them. Then we would put the biscuits in our pockets and go on to the activities of the day.

We usually ate only two meals a day. That's why breakfast was such a big deal. Sometimes biscuits and water were the only things that kept us going between breakfast and dinner. We were always glad Grandmother had the wisdom to make more biscuits than were necessary for breakfast.

I recall one day when, after breakfast, we went to the fields to help Uncle Robert work the sweet potatoes. We had been working for quite some time when I became hungry.

I kept working because I knew Uncle Robert would not let me go back to the house to try to find something that had been left over from breakfast. Then I remembered that I had something to eat right in my pocket. I had one of Grandmother's biscuits.

I reached into my pocket, and there it was, smothered with sweet blackberry preserves. I believe that was the best biscuit I ever had, and I ate it quickly.

As Christians, isn't it good to know that when we become weary and are left wanting by the experiences of life, we have something to help us in our pockets. As the Psalmist says, "Thy word have I hid in mine heart, that I might not sin against Thee." (Psalm 119:11)

Just as I had hidden that biscuit in my pocket, so I hide the Word of God in my heart, and the Word is sweet, too.

The Psalmist continued to tell us about the blackberry preserves on the Word when he wrote, "How sweet are Thy words unto my taste! Yea, sweeter than honey to my mouth!" (Psalm 119:103)

When we become hungry for spiritual sustenance, there is some bread in our hearts.

WORKING THE FIELDS

7

What is an allowance?

As children, we didn't know what an allowance was—we worked because we had to. Young people do not work anymore the way we used to. We worked and we enjoyed working.

Every morning we had our chores to do. Some of us slopped the hogs, others milked the cows, and some churned the butter. I believe the job nobody wanted to do was to chop the cotton.

I remember my grandfather taking us to Mr. Bowie's cotton fields one day. This man had fields so long that we couldn't see to the ends of them. All we could see was the heat rising from the fields.

Mr. Bowie owned a lot of land, and he grew a lot of cotton. We worked Mr. Bowie's field all day long to receive only a quarter at the end of the day. I really didn't like to work Mr. Bowie's fields. I don't think he treated us fairly. I wanted to work our own fields.

My grandfather's fields were not as large as Mr. Bowie's, but we did keep whatever the fields yielded. A good summer with plenty of rain brought a big harvest.

My grandfather planted everything: he planted corn, wheat, cotton, peanuts, sweet potatoes, tomatoes, and anything else that would grow on his land. My favorite was the wheat.

I remember one particular year when I must have been eight years old. My grandfather had grown quite a few acres of wheat and he had a tremendous crop. The pests were not bad that year and there was very little loss of wheat.

After the wheat had been reaped, we went to the mill. It seemed as though we waited there all day while the flour was shaken from the kernels of wheat and collected in burlap sacks. Some of the sacks were 25 pounds, and others were 50 pounds. There were a lot of burlap bags of flour.

The workers at the mill helped us get the bags of flour on the truck and we were on our way home. When we arrived home, there were many bags of flour, but not enough help.

My uncles and cousins had gone to town on business of their own. A storm was blowing up and we had to get the flour off the truck or cover it with something. My grandfather decided to take it off the truck.

My eldest cousin, June Boy, and my grandfather unloaded the truck with little assistance from me. The bags were too heavy for me, but they got the job done.

After they finished unloading the truck and carrying the flour into the house, they were tired. Both flopped down in chairs and went to sleep. The job would have been much easier if there had been more people around to help them.

The harvest was plentiful, but the laborers were few.

One day, when Jesus looked out over the multitudes, He was moved with compassion. The people were scattered abroad, as sheep having no shepherd.

Then He said, "The harvest is plenteous, but the laborers are few; pray ye therefore the Lord of the harvest, that He will send forth laborers into His harvest." (Matthew 9:37–38)

The more the laborers, the easier the load.

ICE CREAM AND BEES

ome summer afternoons seemed to be extra long and extra hot. We would try to find a shade tree where we could sit on the ground, and try not to exert too much energy.

Every now and then, someone would suggest that Grandmother make some ice cream, and everyone else would say, "Amen."

If Grandmother said "yes," we would drive two miles into town to get some ice at the ice house. We would buy a big block of ice, bring it home, and get to work. Someone would bring out the ice cream churn. Someone else would break up the ice. The women would be in the kitchen, making the custard.

I used to enjoy sitting by the side of the churn, watching the grownups prepare it to receive that sweet custard.

When the custard was ready, my grandmother would pour it into the churn, then surround the container with ice and salt. Then, someone else would crank the handle. We could hardly wait for the custard to freeze so we could taste that cool, sweet ice cream on those hot summer days.

One time, after the ice cream was made, a lot of people seemed to materialize out of thin air. Everyone got a tablespoon or two, but all got some.

As my cousin Linda sat under a tree eating her ice cream, bees began to appear around her.

In order to get away from the bees, she jumped up and started running, but they followed her. She was screaming as she ran, and I don't think she lost one drop of that ice cream.

Linda later said she was not going to let those bees get any of her ice cream, because it was too good. Linda loved to eat, and she was not about to share her ice cream with a bee.

She ran inside the house to get away from those bees. That house was her "ark of safety."

God has given us many sweet gifts. We have joy, peace, assurance, His mercy, His faithfulness, and so much more.

We would fare well to follow Linda's example. When the bees come to try to steal our sweet things, let's run into the house, the "ark of safety."

STORM HOLLER

9

The experience of spending much of my youth in Due West, South Carolina, is something for which I am appreciative and grateful.

We learned what work was at an early age. We did everything that we were big enough to do, and we carried out our chores dutifully and respectfully.

We picked fruit, chopped cotton, picked cotton, corn and beans. We dug up sweet potatoes and did whatever else needed to be done. We did it without receiving an allowance.

In our spare time, we would go into the woods, spending lazy summer afternoons playing "hide and seek," or anything else we felt like doing.

My grandparents were the best anyone could have had. My grandfather was a hard worker and a good provider. He could kill a quail without even taking aim.

My grandmother was the sweetest woman that ever lived. She could feed two dozen people with a chicken and some dumplings. She was also the one who sounded the alarm when there was a storm moving in. You could hear her "storm" holler a mile away.

One day, while we were playing in the back pasture on the other side of the woods, we heard her "storm" holler. The sun was shining brightly where we

were playing, but from her viewpoint and experience, she knew the storm was moving in quickly.

When we heard the holler, we all stopped playing and quietly listened in order to make sure it was her.

After the call came again, we all made a mad dash through the woods, running toward the house. We did not want to get caught in the storm.

As we approached the house, the rain began to fall—but we were able to stay ahead of the rain. It was the most curious thing to me to have the sun shining ahead while the rain was falling right behind us. It never caught us.

I believe it didn't catch us because we heard the warning in time. We barely made it to shelter without getting wet, but we made it, and there we stayed until the storm had passed.

Proverbs 18:10 says, "The name of the Lord is a strong tower: the righteous runneth into it, and is safe." It is good to know that in a world where storm clouds are always gathering, the Holy Spirit is still sounding the alarm, and the righteous have a hiding place. The name of the Lord is our place of refuge.

If there is a storm moving in your life, I encourage you to run to the shelter. Remember, "God is our refuge and strength, a very present help in the time of trouble." (Psalm 46:1)

HUSH, THE LORD IS TALKING

My grandparents were deeply religious people. They were also very traditional in their approach to life. They taught us how to be respectful, especially to our elders, and to have respect for the Lord's Day, which was Sunday. On Sunday, all activity ceased. No one labored in any way. Sunday was the day of rest.

There were certain things we did not do. We did not swear, talk back, disobey, and definitely, no temper tantrums. My grandfather had a way of cutting off a peach-tree hickory and using it on our behinds that kept all of the above mentioned in check.

One of the most intriguing and mysterious times for me with my grandparents was whenever a storm would move in. Then, we would all have to come inside the house and sit down quietly in the long center hallway that divided the east rooms from the west.

My grandfather would sit at the head of the hallway, and everyone else would sit or lie along the sides of the hallway. No one made a sound because my grandparents believed that whenever the thunder roared, the Lord was talking.

Believe me when I tell you that no one made a sound, not even the chickens that were under the house. Those moments would sometimes become very frightening for me because I could not interpret what the Lord was saying, and it would scare me to death.

You see, I thought the Lord was trying to tell me something and I wanted to know what it was. Those times when there was an extremely loud burst of thunder, I would try to get under the couch on which I was sitting and hold my ears so I could not hear.

My grandfather would say, "Hush, the Lord is talking."

I can remember thinking, "I wish He would be quiet."

As I recall sitting quietly in the hallway during a thunderstorm, I realize that those were the times that I began to develop a deep reverence for God. The Psalmist wrote, "Be still, and know that I am God." (Psalm 46:10)

I know now that the quiet reverence in the hall was just my family's way of showing respect for God, but I have also learned that it is only when we are quiet and still before Him that He speaks to us.

He speaks in the storm.

In order to hear Him, we must be still ourselves.

Hush Hush

Hush Hush

Hush Hush Hush Hush

Hush Hush Hush Hush

41

THE UPPER ROOM

The big house was a classic. It was a clapboard building that had been whitewashed. The house had a very large screened-in front porch. On the porch sat a rocking chair along with other chairs. I especially enjoyed rocking in that rocking chair.

On entering the front door of the house, one would step into a very long and wide center hallway that divided the east rooms from the west. In it there was an old pump organ, some Victorian-style chairs, and a couch. On the wall hung pictures of my mother's and aunt's college diplomas.

The house rested upon large stones that served as the foundation. The chickens and other yard animals used the space between the rocks and the floor of the house for a shelter when it rained.

The upper room was the place least used in the house. This was the fancy room where the grown folks did their entertaining.

It was furnished with a couch, chairs, and end tables. There were pictures of some of my ancestors. I believe they were my grandfather's mother and my grandmother's father.

In the corner, there was an old upright piano that was my favorite piece of furniture in the entire house. It was on that old out-of-tune upright piano that I first began to play.

One Sunday when I was six or seven years old, we had been to church and the morning hymn was "Come, Thou Almighty King." After we returned home and had eaten dinner, I went into the upper room and began to pick out the tune I had heard in church, and was soon picking out the chords.

My grandfather heard the piano and thought it was my Aunt Gen or Aunt Frances playing. He started to sing, and thinking it was one of his daughters, he said, "Put some more bass in it, Daughter." I didn't know what the bass was, so I just started playing louder.

I don't know if he ever found out that it wasn't one of his daughters playing the piano that day, but I knew who it was. It was me!

From that day forward, I spent as much time as I could in the upper room, playing that old piano. My grandfather was my greatest encouragement at that time, and he never even knew it. He was my encouragement in the upper room.

How many young people do we know that need encouragement? We can encourage them without even knowing we have done so. Too, we can also discourage without knowing what we have done.

It is in the upper room that encouragement is given.

Let's try to make sure that we encourage and not discourage.

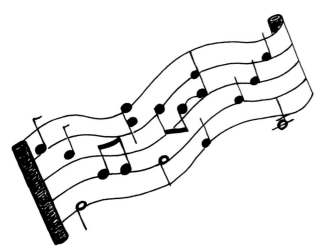

GRANDFATHER'S LEAD

My grandfather had two hunting dogs that I knew. One's name was Lead, and the other was Joe.

Lead was the younger of the two and was loved by everyone. Joe was mean as the devil. I believe the reason he died so mysteriously is that someone fed him poison because he was so mean. Joe was so mean that all the barnyard animals, and even Lead, stayed away from him.

On the other hand, Lead was faithful and true. Lead knew Grandfather's footsteps. Every time Grandfather would step out of a door to the house—front or back door—Lead would be there waiting for him.

I believe Lead would lie under the house and listen for Grandfather's footsteps walking up the hallway. Lead was obedient, dependable, and loyal to my grandfather.

Lead was always anxious to go hunting for rabbits or squirrels with my grandfather. One day, as Grandfather was preparing to go hunting, Lead got so excited that he began leaping off the ground.

Grandfather took my Cousin Willie and me hunting with him that day. We had gone about a mile from the house when Lead took off after something that I couldn't see, but my grandfather did. It was a skunk.

Grandfather tried to call Lead back to him, but Lead had run up to the skunk and had gotten himself sprayed.

Immediately after the skunk sprayed him, Lead began to bite at the air as if there was an unseen enemy attacking him. Then he began to rub his head on the ground and make a coughing noise. I thought he was going to die right there.

Lead took off running, and I really didn't know where he was going.

My grandfather stood there laughing quietly to himself. Then he said softly, "Another lesson learned."

When we arrived back home, we knew Lead was there because we could smell him. He came out to greet us, but we all ran into the house. I don't know what Grandfather did to Lead to get rid of the smell, but it didn't work too well at all.

I don't know how the minds of all animals work, but I do know that a dog must have a good memory. I say this because from that day forward, Lead didn't want to be around anything that had black and white markings. He would even run from black and white chickens.

It is good to remember those things that God has warned us about in His Word. Remember those things that cause pain and avoid them.

Our adversary, the devil, has many skunks in this world, just waiting to spray someone. Let's avoid those things that we know will leave a stench on us.

48

A DOG NAMED PRINCE

magine this. I was about 13 years old. I had wanted a dog of my own for quite some time. My grandfather had his dogs. My uncles had their dogs. And I wanted my own.

One special day, my mother took me with her into town to do some banking. As she stood in line waiting to be helped by the teller, an older white lady came into the bank. She had not come to conduct any business. She had come to give something away.

The bank was not very crowded, but there were people there taking care of their business.

I was sitting in the chair by the door when the woman came in. I noticed her right away. She was smartly dressed in a gray suit. Her hair was silver gray and very neat. Even as a child, I could discern that this woman was not poor.

She spoke very loudly with a strong southern accent. "Does anyone here want a dog? My husband and I mated two pure-white German shepherd dogs and all the puppies came out colored. We've got one colored puppy left. Does anyone want him?"

I immediately sprang from my seat and told my mother I wanted the dog.

My mother turned and told the lady that we would take him, and asked

where the dog was. The lady told my mother that she would bring the dog to us, and then proceeded to ask for directions to our place.

I left the bank so excited that I didn't know what to do.

When we arrived home, I told everyone what had happened at the bank.

A few days passed and the woman had not brought the dog. I was beginning to doubt that she would bring it.

Then, after a full week had passed, a car pulled off the highway into our driveway. I just knew it had to be her. The car stopped and it was the silver gray haired lady from the bank.

She got out of the car with a silver gray puppy in her arms. She proceeded to tell us that this was the runt of the litter. I didn't care. This dog was mine!

As soon as she placed the puppy in my arms, it wiggled and fell to the ground. Then it ran under the house. I thought that he was afraid of strangers. I tried everything I could to get him to come to me, but he wouldn't come.

My grandmother told me that when he got hungry enough he would come. The next day he came out from under the house and I was able to feed and pet him. But he was still very nervous.

He remained unsure of me for a week. Then one day I realized something was wrong with him. He was running around the house coughing and hitting his snout with his paw. I went to him and turned him over. Inside his jaws there was a chicken bone stuck to the roof of his mouth. I reached in and pulled it out.

He was so happy that I pulled that bone out that he jumped all over me and began to lick my face. I had finally won him over, and that day I named him "Prince."

After that, Prince and I were inseparable. He protected me. He lay by my feet. He would bark and growl at anyone who came close to me—except my grandmother. He was truly my best buddy.

I remember that my cousins wanted to see just how far Prince would go in protecting me. They proceeded to wrestle with me and playfully punch me around. Suddenly, the hair on the back of his neck rose up and Prince stood on his feet with a very menacing snarl on his lips.

Prince was about three months old at that time, and no longer a little puppy. He took off after my cousins as they began to run and scream for help, but it was too late. Prince was mad.

One of my cousins climbed on top of the old gas tank. Another climbed on top of the smokehouse. The third one hid in the outhouse. I couldn't help because I was too busy laughing at all of them. They never disturbed me again when Prince was around.

Prince appreciated me because I removed that chicken bone from his mouth. How much more should we appreciate God for what He has done for us. He removed the power of sin in our lives, by sending His only Son to the cross.

Let's show God how much we appreciate Him.

OLD DELLA

ut of all the animals on the farm, Della was the most intriguing. Della was my grandfather's mule. She was ugly and had a sway back, but she was a good plowing mule.

I remember my cousins and I had a lot of mischievous fun with Della because she spooked so easily. We would sneak up behind her and make a loud noise and she would take off running.

Sometimes I believe that mule could communicate with my grandfather, because every time we would spook her or shoot her behind with our BB guns, she would always run for Grandfather. If she found him, she would have this "tattle-tale" look on her face as she would look back in our direction, and Grandfather always knew we had done something to her.

The most interesting thing about Della was her homing instinct. Every spring that crazy mule would jump the fence of the pasture and run ten miles up the road to the farm where she was born.

My grandfather would gather up all of his grandsons and we would have to walk ten miles up the road to find her, rope her, and bring her back home.

The point is, Della knew that our home was not her home and she wanted to go home.

The place where she was born was a pasture filled with mean bulls and

big horses. The place scared me because the bulls always came running after us whenever we entered the pasture. I spent more time watching out for the bulls than searching for Della.

After we would bring Della back to our home, my grandfather would tie her to a pole in the barn and leave her there for a few days until she settled back in.

Della was like a part of the family, but she always had that strong desire to go back to the place she thought was home.

Sometimes she would stand and gaze off into the distance, as if she was longing for home. She did that until the day she died.

God's Word says that we who are Christians are sojourning here on Earth. This world is not our home, and many times we find ourselves longing for heaven and home.

Our citizenship is in heaven. As long as we keep our focus on home, our priorities will be in the right place. While we are here, let's remember the words of a great hymn:

"Guide me, O Thou great Jehovah,
  Pilgrim through this barren land;
  I am weak, but Thou art mighty,
  Hold me with Thy powerful hand:
  Bread of Heaven,
  Feed me till I want no more."

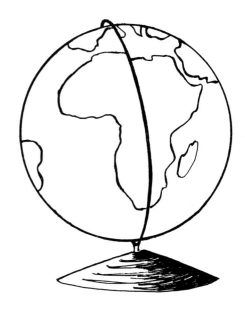

THE CHAIN GANG

15

We were outside, shooting tin cans with our BB guns, when we heard a thumping noise down by the highway.

At first, the sound was faint and muffled by the roar of car engines speeding down the road.

After a few hours, the thumping sound was very near. We ran around to the front of the house to be greeted by a most curious sight.

There were fifteen men dressed in red and white striped uniforms. These men were chained together at their ankles. They were using big sledge hammers to break up the highway.

The men were being guarded by two white police officers, both of them carrying shotguns. What we saw frightened us, but we were fascinated and continued to stare at those men.

As they worked, they sang a song. I don't remember what the song was, but it seemed to help them keep some kind of cadence.

My grandmother came out of the house and stood on the front porch. She said, "There goes the chain gang. Don't you boys ever get in trouble or they may put you on the chain gang."

The sun was hot. The men were chained at the ankle and their skin was dark from baking in the hot sun all day long. I remember thinking that I never

wanted to be on the chain gang. It didn't seem to be much fun at all.

We watched until they disappeared on the other side of the rise at the fork of the road. The sight of those men haunted me for many days afterward. I could only imagine how terrible it must have been for them to be in that kind of bondage, with guards watching them to insure that they didn't escape. The only thing that seemed to get them through the work was the song they sang, and the cadence they kept.

Most—if not all—of us have been a part of a spiritual chain gang at some point in our lives. We were chained and bound to something to which we really did not want to belong.

Some of us are bound to something right now to which we do not want to belong. We are being kept and watched by unseen guards and we don't know how to break free.

Well, I have some good news. The Scripture says, "No man can enter into a strong man's house, and spoil his goods, except he will first bind the strong man; and then he will spoil his house." (Mark 3:27)

Listen, you may be bound to something right now, and the strong man called the devil is guarding you, but there is a stronger man in the house. His name is Jesus. He can set you free. He came to set you and me free.

Stop breaking up your road.

Let us take these chains to the Man who is able to break them.

Jesus is His name.

AUNT MAE DAVIS

16

"Whippoorwill."

"Whippoorwill."

Whenever we heard a soprano voice singing "Whippoorwill," coming up the hill that lay between Uncle Robert's home and the big house, we knew it had to be Aunt Mae Davis. (I don't know why we used her entire name whenever we referred to her.)

Mae Davis was a classic. Her head was always covered with a scarf or a hat, and she wore ankle length dresses. She laughed loud, talked loud, and just seemed to enjoy life.

Aunt Mae Davis had the hands of a woman who knew what hard work was. Her face was etched with character, and her back was slightly bent, probably from stooping in the fields, working most of her life.

Mae Davis was my grandfather's only sister. They were extremely close. It seems as though I can still hear my grandmother saying, "Kid, here comes Mae Davis." (My grandmother sometimes referred to my grandfather as "Kid.")

All of us would be excited to see Aunt Mae Davis come up the hill, because she was so much fun to be around.

Mae Davis lived about a mile away. Her house sat above the ground upon large rocks, and it was covered with gray asphalt shingles. Since her husband,

63

Uncle Marsh, had passed away, she lived with her son, Jeff Davis, and her daughter, Alice. Alice's children, Bubba and Needa, also lived there.

Her house always had a slight musky odor because her son, Jeff, was mentally handicapped and sometimes he didn't clean himself properly. However, she cared for Jeff until her dying day.

There were not any homes that cared for the mentally handicapped, and there were not any assistance programs. It was the responsibility of the family to care for their own. That is exactly what Mae Davis did.

Mae Davis was a strong woman. She always had a smile on her face and a song in her heart. She loved music, and whenever I went to visit her, she would always say, "Play me a piece on the piano," and I would gladly grant her wish. As I would play, she would sit there and sing along, even if she didn't know the words—she would make some up.

One day—after I had gotten a spanking for chasing the chickens—I was sitting crying on Aunt Mae Davis' porch when she came out of the house.

She looked down at me and then she looked up as if she was seeing something that I could not see.

She had been standing there for a while before she looked down at me and said, "Be happy, child, Aunt Mae loves you." Then she turned around and went back inside the house.

I have often thought about that day and those words, "Be happy, child, Aunt Mae loves you." I believe that if Aunt Mae Davis could be happy with everything she had to endure, then I should be able to be happy, too.

She saw joy in everything. Maybe she understood what James wrote of when he said, "Count it all joy when ye fall into divers temptations; knowing this, that the trying of your faith worketh patience." (James 1:2–3)

Mae Davis tried to find the good in everything.

We'd fare well to do the same.

SNAKE IN THE SHED

17

It was a typical weekday afternoon. The hogs had been slopped. The cows had been milked. The butter had been churned. The water had been drawn from the well and we were preparing to go down to the tree house.

We were playing behind Uncle Ollie's house, in front of his tool shed, when Uncle Ollie came out of the house to get something from the shed.

I was excited to see Uncle Ollie walking toward the shed because when he opened the door I could enjoy the pleasurable smell of the feed and corn inside. The aromas gave me a homey feeling.

As Uncle Ollie began to open the shed, the dogs started barking and looking at the ground near the door. Suddenly, I saw Uncle Ollie leap into the air and let out a sound somewhere between hysteria and shock. He leaped so high that I could imagine what Jack looked like when he jumped over the candlestick.

When Uncle Ollie came down out of the air, he yelled, "Snake! Run!"

We had been taught to stay away from snakes, and when he said "Snake," it didn't matter how big it was or how small, or what kind it was; all we heard was "danger!"

My grandfather and Uncle Ollie had what they called "snake sticks." These were really tree limbs that had been carved or shaped to have a large

67

blunt end which would be used to strike the heads of snakes. Uncle Ollie's snake stick was leaning on the side of the shed, but the snake scared him so badly, he forgot about the stick and took off running.

Once we had all put a respectful distance between ourselves and the snake, we turned around to see what was going on.

One of the dogs lunged threateningly at the snake, while the others just barked and backed away. The snake had already curled up to defend itself when Uncle Ollie saw the snake stick leaning against the side of the shed.

As quickly and quietly as he could, Uncle Ollie ran to the side of the shed and grabbed the stick. He cautiously approached the snake, then began to hit it with the thick end of the stick as if he had lost his mind. I imagine the creature was dead after the first blow, but my uncle continued to hit that snake until he wore his arms out.

I don't know what kind of snake it was, but I do know that when Uncle Ollie finished with it, the creature didn't look much like a snake at all. He beat the stuffing out of that snake.

In the Word of God, Satan is described as a snake, and he is an expert at surprising the people of God. Many times when we go to our sheds to get our tools of faith, Satan jumps out, trying to distract us from doing what God has told us to do.

Remember that when he jumps out, you have a "snake stick" in the Word of God.

James 4:7 reads, "Submit to God. Resist the devil, and he will flee from you." It is good to know that we don't have to run from the old serpent anymore.

If we resist him, he will flee from us.

KINGDOMS MADE OF SAND 18

s a child, one of my favorite things to do was build castles out of wet sand after it rained. As soon as the rain stopped falling, I would rush outside and get busy.

One day, after I had just finished building an impressive-looking little city of sand in the middle of the sandy road that lay between my grandparents' home and Uncle Ollie's, I was to learn a valuable lesson.

My Uncle Ollie drove up the road in his pickup truck and ran right over my little city of sand. Unknowingly, he flattened the whole thing, and I was so hurt.

I thought I had built something that I could enjoy forever, when in reality, all that was there had been sand that could be washed away.

The third chapter of Paul's letter to the Philippians lets us know that at one point in his life, the Apostle was building for himself a kingdom that looked very impressive. But, after his experience with Christ, he said in verse 7, "But what things were gain to me, those I counted loss for Christ."

In Exodus, we read that Pharaoh thought he had a great kingdom, until God showed him who was really in control. In Daniel, chapter 5, we read that Belshazzar thought he had a great kingdom until he saw the handwriting on the wall.

Charlemagne, King of the Franks, crowned Emperor of Rome, had riches and wealth unimaginable. However, for a man who ruled such a vast kingdom and controlled such great wealth, he left strict and strange instructions for his memorial service.

Charlemagne was to be propped up on his throne, with his crown on his head, with his royal robes adorning his body.

As the mourners filed into the great cathedral to view his body for the last time, they noticed a book in his hand. Drawing closer, they recognized the book to be a Bible.

The dead king's fingers were pointing to one verse in that Bible. That verse was Mark 8:36, "For what shall it profit a man if he gains the whole world, and loses his own soul?" Evidently, this man realized that all of his fame, wealth and power was only for a season.

There are properties of sand that I learned about the hard way when I was a child.

Sand cannot stand on its own.

Sand cannot be held in the hand without slipping through.

Sand can be blown by the wind, and washed away by the rain.

A truck can flatten a sand city.

Many people have spent great amounts of money, long hours, and even their health and relationships trying to build kingdoms that are made out of sand.

There is nothing wrong with aspiring to be great; nothing wrong with having money, or a good occupation and position in life. But when your desires begin to take priority over your relationship with Jesus Christ, you begin to operate on shaky ground.

Let's try to make sure that the kingdom that we build has eternal value, that it is built upon the gospel of Jesus Christ. As Jesus said, "Upon this rock I will build My church, and the gates of hell shall not prevail against it." (Matthew 16:18)

Remember, only what you do for Christ will last.

TREE HOUSE AT THE EDGE OF THE WOODS

y two closest buddies were my cousins, Willie and Johnny. Of course, there were Frederick and Bubba, too, but Fred was much younger and Bubba lived a good distance from us and we didn't see him every day.

Willie and Johnny had built a tree house at the edge of the woods, right next to the hog pen. In the summer, it was our favorite meeting place. They had nailed strips of wood to the side of the tree to make the tree house more accessible, but the wood that they used was old and rotten.

Whenever we went to the tree house, I usually stayed on the ground because I wasn't sure that once I got up in it I would be able to get back down.

Many times we would hide from Bubba, because Bubba seemed crazy to us. Although the tree house was our favorite hiding place, I was afraid to climb up into it.

One day when we were hiding from Bubba, he found our secret place and we had to climb up into the tree house so he wouldn't see us.

We sat up there very quietly, while he called our names. I heard him call up from the ground, "I know where y'all are. Y'all's up in that tree house."

Before I knew it, I had yelled back, "No, we ain't. We're somewhere else."

75

I thought I had done the right thing. But that was before I felt Willie slap me on the side of the head. By that time, Bubba was on his way up. You could have bought me for a penny, but it was too late. Bubba was coming on in.

The tree house was only large enough for the three of us and when Bubba came in, it began to fall apart. All of us began to yell and scream.

I looked for a branch to grab to keep myself from falling. I managed to climb out of what was left of the tree house onto a large branch.

As things began to settle down, I could see that everyone was safe. They were beginning to climb down the tree. Everyone except me. I was terrified and didn't know how to get down out of that tree.

I began to ask for help. Johnny told me to get down the same way I had gotten up. But, without the tree house, everything looked different.

I sat there, looking down at Willie and Johnny beating up Bubba, and I decided to stay there because I thought I might be next.

Bubba ran off with Willie in hot pursuit of him. Johnny stayed there trying to decide if he was going to help me get down or leave me to my own devices.

After a while, he asked, "How did you get up there?"

I said I climbed up. He responded by saying I should climb back down.

I remember saying to myself, "I can do it. I can do it. I can do it. I can do it. I can do it."

I began to carefully put my feet on lower branches and Johnny kept saying, "Come on, you can do it."

It seemed as though it took me forever, but I finally made it back to the ground and felt a sense of accomplishment. When I looked back up the tree at the remains of the house, it really was not all that high up and I felt kind of stupid.

There will be those times when we feel as though we are up in a tree, out on a limb, and cannot get down. But with faith in God, we really can get back down.

You are not as high up in the tree as it seems, and you can do it. "I can do all things through Christ who strengthens me." (Philippians 4:13)

GOING FISHING WITH JOHNNY AND W.B.

t was through my experience of going fishing with my cousin, Johnny, and his friend, W.B., that I really began to believe that Peter walked on the water.

W.B. was tall and skinny, with a head that looked, to my young eyes, to be three feet long. He had a way of talking that reminded me of an old steam locomotive pulling away from the train station. He would begin talking very slowly and deeply, but by the time he was midway through his narrative, he was talking so fast and high I really had to concentrate on what he was saying to understand him.

Every time W.B. would begin to talk, I had to turn my head and look away from him. I couldn't look at him and listen to him at the same time without laughing.

One day, as we were walking to the fishing hole, W.B. was monopolizing the conversation. He was bragging about his fishing ability and he told us, "Y'all ain't gonna catch no big feesh, 'cause they's all waitin' fo me." Then he would fall down laughing.

When we arrived at my cousin Charlie's pond, the water was beautiful. We looked for a perfect spot to drop our lines. As we looked, we saw an old rotten

boat partially hidden in the reeds that grew along the side of the pond.

W.B. said, "I'm gonna get in that boat and catch me some feesh."

Johnny said, "W.B., I wouldn't get in that boat if I was you. That boat looks rotten."

W.B. replied, "You jest don't want me to catch no feesh," and he proceeded to make his way toward the boat. W.B. found a couple of paddles and cautiously got into the boat.

By the way, W.B. could not swim.

He pushed off from shore and was soon in the middle of the pond with his line in the water.

Johnny and I were already catching some pretty nice-sized blue gills when we hear a crash and a loud screech.

We looked up and saw that one of the sides of the boat had fallen off and W.B. was in the water. Suddenly, we saw him rise up out of the water with his legs and feet moving so fast we could barely see them. He was actually running across the top of the water, screaming, "Help me, Jesus! Help me, Lawd!"

W.B. made it to shore, but his troubles were not over. He fell into a bush that was covered with fire ants and they began stinging him wherever they could.

He jumped up and started running toward us, yelling that the devil was after him. By this time, Johnny and I were so frightened we dropped our poles and started running away from him.

W.B. ran back into the water at the shallow end of the pond and began to roll around in the mud. We thought he had lost his mind and we kept our distance.

After a little while, we realized what had happened and we helped him out of the water. He stood there covered with mud and welts from the sting of the ants.

Johnny said, "I told you not to get in that boat."

The first thing W.B. said was, "Y'all tried to kill me."

We had done nothing, but I guess he needed someone to blame.

I find it amazing that many times people blame others for the bad decisions they make themselves.

Maybe we need to pray as did the Psalmist, "Search me, O God, and know my heart: try me, and know my thoughts: and see if there be any wicked way in me, and lead me in the way everlasting." (Psalm 139:23–24)

It just might be that you're the one with the problem.

AN OPEN SEPTIC TANK

21

Believe it when I tell you that all frogs are not princes in disguise.

I was playing hide-and-go-seek with my Cousin Willie. We were playing by the side of Uncle Ollie's house when I noticed a small pool of murky brown water over behind the shed. I had never seen this pool of water before, so I decided to investigate it.

As I approached the pool, there was a heavy, strange smell, but that didn't deter me from my investigation. I noticed a couple of toads jumping around the water and I wanted to catch one of them.

Willie had gone into the house to do some chores and I had time to kill, so I began to chase the toads.

As I proceeded to bend down to grab one of them, I slipped and went into that water, head first. I couldn't get out because the sides of it were steep and the grass surrounding it was slippery.

I began to call for my Cousin Willie. Finally, he came out of the house and began to look for me.

He looked in the shed, under the house, and around the house. I kept screaming, "I'm in the water!" but he didn't believe me.

Finally, he came around the side of the shed and there I was, covered with gook.

Willie screamed, "Boy, you done fell in the septic tank!" I didn't know what a septic tank was. All I knew was that it didn't smell very good. My uncle had been doing some repair on the system and had intentionally left it open until he finished working on it.

Willie grabbed a branch that had fallen from the peach tree and handed it to me. "Grab on," he said.

I grabbed it and he pulled me out, but kept his distance. I just did not know why.

Of all days, on this one my grandmother had to be entertaining company. Her cousins, the Valentines, had come over for a visit and, just as we arrived at the big house, she was pouring them each a glass of lemonade.

They were all sitting outside, under the pecan tree. When Willie told her what had happened, she looked as if she could have rolled over and died right there. Looking back, I know now that she had to have been embarrassed.

My grandmother made me take off my clothes right there, in the presence of all of those ladies. She washed me off outside, using a hose and some Lysol. I smelled so bad that the dogs wouldn't come near me and the rooster ceased to crow.

Later that day, after her company had left, Grandmother asked me how I happened to fall into the septic tank. I told her I had been chasing a toad.

She said, "Boy, didn't I tell you to leave those toads alone?"

I said, "Yes, Grandmother."

She told me that bad things happen to children that don't obey. Believe me when I tell you that I learned a very valuable lesson that day. I learned to stay away from septic tanks, whether they are open or closed.

After that day, I never went close to that spot again, and I began to have a strong dislike for toads.

Satan has many open septic tanks in this world, and he knows how to present the right kind of bait to get the attention of his prey.

The Word of God warns us that if we don't want to fall into a stinking mess, we had better leave those toads alone.

CONDEMNED BUILDINGS

22

A little boy ran into his mother's arms and cried, "Mother, I've just seen a big gorilla in the front yard!"

When his mother looked out of the window, she saw that what her son had taken for a gorilla was really the large black dog that lived next door.

We can't always go by appearances. If we judge just by appearance, we would be apt to say that many people are beyond help. There are many drowning people in this world because they have rejected the lifeguard.

The world has always tried to find a purpose for life other than Jesus Christ. This is because of the world's rejection of the simplicity of the Gospel of Christ. The Apostle Paul wrote to Corinth and said in II Corinthians 11:3, "I am afraid, lest as the serpent deceived Eve by his craftiness, your minds should be led astray from the simplicity and purity of devotion to Christ."

One day, when we were children, my cousins and I were walking through the woods and came across an old building that looked as though it had been abandoned many years earlier.

The wooden planks were rotting and some of them seemed to be falling off the structure. We could tell that it used to be somebody's home. Now, there were vines growing up the sides of the building. It looked as though it was

beyond repair. The building frightened me and I wouldn't get too close to it.

Another day, while walking through that same part of the woods, we were startled to see smoke coming out of the chimney of that old building. Then we saw a man coming out of the door.

He came out, got some wood, and went back inside. To our amazement, the building was still being used.

Someone had seen the value of that old building in the middle of the woods.

If we think back, reflecting on times past, I am sure that at one point or another in our lives we felt like condemned buildings, but God saw the value in us.

Listen, God can fix anything. Nothing is too hard for God. It does not matter how useless we may think we are.

Remember, God is an expert at repairing broken-down, feeling-useless people. He can take a little and make much from it.

I HATE THAT YELLOW BUS 23

Imagine having the time of your life—running through the fields, playing in the woods with your cousins and friends, eating watermelon, and all the fruit you could wish, fishing . . . just plain loving life. Then, one day, it all suddenly ends.

When we moved from South Carolina to Cleveland, Ohio, it was devastating to me. I hated the big city. For one thing, there were no fishing holes. A saving grace was that every summer we would head back home on the first smoking thing moving south.

We would board the B&O in Cleveland, and go to Washington, D.C., where we would change trains. I never appreciated Washington, although we usually had to stay over for a few days.

My Aunt Margaret and Uncle Craig lived in Washington. It seemed as though everywhere they lived there, it was behind, in front, or at the side of a cemetery or funeral home. I couldn't wait to leave.

Sometimes we would leave the same day that we had arrived. But there were other times that we had to lay over and spend a few days with my aunt and uncle.

On the day we were scheduled to leave, my Uncle Craig would take us to Washington's Union Station, where we would board the Silver Comet. I loved

91

that train. It was a part of the Seaboard train line. There was the Silver Meteor, the Silver Star, and the Silver Comet.

The Comet originated at Penn Station in Manhattan, New York. That was where my Aunt Lee and her children would board. We would join them on the same train when it reached Washington.

The Comet would leave Washington at 5:15 p.m., and would arrive in Abbeville, South Carolina, at 5:50 a.m. My grandparents would be there to meet us, along with my uncles with the trucks to carry our luggage.

It was always a joyous reunion. To me, it marked the beginning of a three-month stay in heaven, because I was home with Grandmother.

All summer long there was one adventure after another. Good times abounded, so you can understand why this was heaven for me.

June and July would roll by, but when August came, I would sense that the good times would soon come to an end. It was time for school to begin.

On one August morning, while I was pursuing my favorite activity, "chasing the chickens," I looked up to see a yellow bus coming down the road. It stopped in front of the long driveway that ran by my Uncle Ollie's house to the highway.

My cousins ran from the house and down the driveway. Then they boarded the bus and it took them away. I was hurt because it didn't take me.

Where was that bus going that I couldn't go? There was no one to play with all day long. I had to make up fun for myself, but that wasn't as enjoyable without my cousins.

Each morning after that, the same bus showed up and took them away. I noticed that my mother was beginning to pack our luggage. It was time for us to go back to Cleveland.

As we left the house one late summer evening, going to the train station in Abbeville, my heart felt as though it was breaking. It was torn in two. I had to leave my grandmother, but I didn't want Mama to leave *me* behind.

Mama wouldn't have let me stay regardless of how much I protested. Cleveland was beckoning and I had to answer.

The writer of Ecclesiasties might have experienced something similar and then have come to an understanding that "To every thing there is a season, and a time to every purpose under heaven." (Ecclesiasties 3:1)

My time with my grandparents and cousins was over for that summer. My only response to a broken heart was to learn to look forward to the next summer, and reflect on the good times of the past.

IT SEEMED BEAUTIFUL . . . FROM A DISTANCE

 he setting was just north of Jacksonville, Florida, near the Georgia border. It was exactly 7:01 a.m. I will never forget the time because of what happened.

I was driving the car—the Blue Goose—while my fraternity brother, Charles, slept. We were on our way back to school after our spring break. We had spent the entire week fishing in Florida. We were traveling on Highway 1.

Near the border, there was a small lake that was barely visible because of the vegetation surrounding it. But, with the early morning mist rising off of it, boy, it did look beautiful and promising.

I pulled the Blue Goose over, just as Charles was waking up, wondering why I had stopped.

When I pointed out the lake to him, with its water as smooth as glass and fish jumping in it, Charles leaped out of the car and had his fishing equipment ready before I even opened my door.

We proceeded to the lake with our tackle, lures, worms, and cooler. We disregarded the "No Trespassing" sign and kept on trudging toward the lake.

It was beautiful. Just ahead of us was a patch of the most beautiful flowers I had ever seen, and about ten yards ahead of the flowers was the lake.

Charles and I stepped into the patch of flowers at the same time. They seemed to be growing up out of firm ground. To our surprise, we both found ourselves in quicksand up to our knees.

That should have been enough to send us scurrying back to the car. But, because we were determined to catch fish, we pulled ourselves out and proceeded to the lake.

My first cast landed a four-pound bass. Charles landed a two-pounder on his second cast. We were ready for some serious fishing when I looked down and found myself surrounded by four aggressive-looking water moccasins—the smallest was about four-feet long and all of them had their mouths open, revealing a white lining and strong fangs. By this time, Charles had a problem of his own. He was being stalked by an eight-foot alligator.

The closest snake was about seven feet from me, so I managed to pick up a fallen tree limb and brush them all out of the way.

Charles was already heading toward the car with the gator not too far behind. Praise God, we both made it to the car unharmed. We were shaken up, but unharmed.

Tony Bennett may have left his heart in San Francisco, but we left our stomachs, kidneys, livers, bladders—and a few other things I would rather not mention—by the side of that lake.

There is a lesson I learned from that experience. Every time I see a warning or a "No Trespassing" sign, I take heed . . . especially those found in the Word of God.

You know, with all of those "Thou shalt not's," there are reasons why God has instructed us not to do certain things. He knows that not everything that looks good, *is*.

"Shalt not's" include that beautiful woman who tries to lure a man away from his home and family; that handsome man who only wants to use the unsuspecting woman; that white powder that is killing and destroying people; even those chitterlings people with high blood pressure and heart problems are not supposed to eat.

The fruit looked good to Adam and Eve, but see what happened when they ate it. Bathsheba looked good to King David, but his sin with her followed him the rest of his life.

There is another, more personal lesson. From a distance, we're beautiful people. We may look well-dressed, with a nice smile, friendly, and may seem to be under control, having it all together. But when someone gets close, they begin to see all of the insecurities, the quicksand, the gators, and the snakes that are a part of our make-up.

Maybe that is why the Word of God tells us that He scrutinizes our paths. Darkness and light are alike to Him; not one thing is hidden. And guess what? He still loves us enough to allow us to work on removing those things that ought not be there.

He loves you.

Who loves you?

Jesus Loves You.

ONE MATCH CAN DESTROY A LOT OF TREES

25

"**...N**ow if we put bits into the horses' mouths so that they may obey us, we direct their entire body as well. Behold, the ships also, though they are so great and are driven by strong winds, are still directed by a very small rudder, going wherever the inclination of the pilot desires. So also the tongue is a small part of the body, and yet it boasts of great things. Behold, how great a forest is set aflame by such a small fire!" (James 3:3–5)

I was born in South Carolina, and much of my youth was spent playing in the woods that surrounded my grandparents' farm. In those woods were many different kinds of trees. Some of them were very tall and large pine trees. Then there were stately pecan and black walnut trees. There were also maple, oak, cypress, peach, pear, apple, and various other kinds of trees growing on my grandparents' land.

These trees offered shade from the intense heat of the sun. These trees provided fruit. Sometimes muscadine vines would wrap themselves around the trees and produce fruit. Birds nested in the trees. Squirrels found a home in them. We would climb them and build tree houses. These trees were a gift to many different creatures.

Sometimes during a storm, a bolt of lightning might strike a tree and destroy it. When a tree falls in the forest, it will often fall on another tree and damage it also. If the woods are dry, an entire forest can be destroyed by one bolt of lightning.

A group of people can be compared to a forest. They all have different personalities, produce different fruit, have different functions, and when they unite their abilities can perform great tasks, getting a lot accomplished. However, some people are like bolts of lightning, seeming to enjoy burning trees with their tongues.

If we call ourselves Christians, then we should remember what James says in 3:8–12: "But no one can tame the tongue; it is a restless evil and full of deadly poison. With it we bless our Lord and Father; and with it we curse men, who have been made in the likeness of God; from the same mouth come both blessing and cursing. My brethren, these things ought not to be this way. Does a fountain send out from the same opening both fresh and bitter water? Can a fig tree, my brethren, produce olives, or a vine produce figs? Neither can salt water produce fresh."

We need to always restrain our tongues and be careful what we say about others. Many people have been hurt and sent to the depths of despair by a lying tongue. Families and churches have been divided because of a gossiping tongue. Great ministries have been wrecked.

Let's use our tongues to bless the Lord and encourage our friends.

Let us speak out against evil and not against people.

That is what God has called us to do.

The author in a more sophisticated pose.